A Soccer Summer Dream
With The Milwaukee Torrent

Written by Marla McKenna
Illustrated by Brenda Kato

Message From the Owner

Dedication and commitment, determination and sacrifice, trust and responsibility, honesty and personal accountability, teamwork and communication, goal setting and risk-taking, mental toughness and physical fitness. These words describe strong leaders, solid citizens and healthy communities.

It is critical, in this day and age, that these attributes be developed in our youth and there is no better place to do so than on the athletic field. Unfortunately, financial support in many of our schools is shrinking for athletics and other so-called extracurricular activities and there is nothing "extra" about the lessons learned through athletics. They are essential.

And that is why the Milwaukee Torrent Community Foundation was established, to nurture the values and attributes that positively impact children and their families by providing educational athletic opportunities to youth through the game of soccer.

The game of soccer (or football as I learned it growing up) has instilled these values in both my players and I, and together as a community we can continue to grow them in the kids who attend.

Coach Andreas Davi

This book belongs to:

Copyright © 2018 by Marla McKenna

All rights reserved. No part of this book may be reproduced or transmitted in any form or by any means, electronic or mechanical, including photocopying, recording, or by any information storage and retrieval system, without permission in writing from the copyright owner.

This is a work of fiction. Names, characters, places and incidents either are the product of the author's imagination or are used fictitiously, and any resemblance to any actual persons, living or dead, events, or locales is entirely coincidental.

Published by Nico 11 Publishing & Design
Quantity order requests can be emailed to:
mike@nico11publishing.com

Author: Marla McKenna
A Soccer Summer Dream With The Milwaukee Torrent

Illustrations, Cover & Interior Layout: Brenda Kato
Visit www.brendakato.com

Editor: Griffin Mill
Author Photo by Julia McKenna

ISBN-13: 978-1945907272

SALES Categories:
Children's Books | Sports & Outdoors | Soccer
Children's Books | Growing Up & Facts of Life | Friendship, Social Skills & School Life | Self-Esteem & Self-Respect
Children's Books | Growing Up & Facts of Life | Family | Siblings

BISAC Codes:
JUV032150 | JUVENILE FICTION | SPORTS & RECREATION | SOCCER
SPO000000 | SPORTS & RECREATION | GENERAL
SPO0400000 SPORTS & RECREATION | SOCCER

Dedication

I am grateful to God for His divine opportunities.

To all kids running after your dreams...
GO FOR IT!

Thank you to the Milwaukee Torrent and special thanks to
Owner and Head Coach, Andy Davi. We just happened to
meet on the set of Milwaukee's own television show,
The Morning Blend, and he invited me to write this book.
I'm so grateful for his inspiration and belief in me.
GO TORRENT!!

- Marla

Thank you to God and my inner circle of family
and friends that support my creative projects.

- Brenda

I dribbled the ball intensely, looking to my left, glancing to my right. I took a shot, fiercely kicking it as it took flight, soaring in the air and clearing the net.

GOAL! WE WON!

The goalie didn't have a chance. My teammates all jumped in victory and excitement, high fives flying everywhere.

My little sister was the first one to greet me as I was carried off the field. She's pretty cool as far as sisters go. Alexandra, I call her Alex for short, she's my twin, just a few minutes younger. She was my first soccer buddy running drills together, kicking the ball back and forth. She's my biggest fan.

"You rock D!" shouted Alex. That's what she calls me, D, short for Dylan.

Alex is an awesome soccer player, and I mean fast. She's also a really great writer, creative and smart. This came in handy when she entered the Milwaukee Torrent essay contest for the chance to be part of the ball crew for the championship game. I mean, how cool would that be? Alex and I both thought it would be absolutely amazing! We love of our hometown professional outdoor soccer team!

The Milwaukee Torrent really care about their fans and the community, and they make the game of soccer so much fun to be around. We really look up to this incredible team.

We met owner and head coach, Andy Davi, and all the players at their welcome party. It was so much fun to get photos that night too. And that's where Alex entered the contest.

It had been a few weeks. We should find out soon if she won.

Jumping off the bus, Alex and I raced to the house. It was a toss-up on who would win depending on which one of us got a head start, but like I said, Alex was fast. When we got to the front door, Mom was waiting for us, waving her hand and holding a beautiful, bright blue envelope from the Milwaukee Torrent. It held the answer to the biggest question we had been patiently waiting for...did Alex win the contest?

It felt like we needed a drum roll or something. Alex was so nervous, and I tried to hide my excitement a bit as she handed me the envelope with only a half-smile on her face. She gave me the honor. I normally would have ripped it open in record time, but this was different. It was sealed with a gold Milwaukee Torrent emblem, and it appeared to be very official.

As I carefully opened the envelope and slowly peeked inside, my eyes grew very large, and I must have given the secret away. Alex quickly grabbed the winning announcement from my grasp and screamed, "We did it!" I loved how she shared the credit with me even though she wrote the essay. "Of course, I pick you D," she shouted to me.

"Mom, we won, and I can pick ten friends to be the ball boys and girls with me. I pick D first! I'm so excited! We are going to be ON THE FIELD WITH THE MILWAUKEE TORRENT AT THEIR CHAMPIONSHIP GAME! I cannot wait! D, we need to tell our soccer team and all our friends at school. Mom, do you think Grandma and Grandpa will come watch us too?" asked Alex.

"I'm sure everyone will be there, and they won't want to miss it," Mom said. Alex was so excited, and so was I!

"This is a once in a life time dream come true," I told Alex. And this time, my sister rocked. I gave her a fist bump, and then we shared our secret handshake. I couldn't wait to tell Dad and my coach. The ball crew had special summer practice sessions with the Torrent before the big game. We needed to practice hard, work smart, and believe in ourselves.

The months flew by, and game day was finally here! The Milwaukee Torrent were about to face their biggest rival. We arrived at Hart Park, and Alex and I had special VIP passes to enter the locker room before the game. That was so cool! When it was finally time to go on the field, we all lined up.

I asked Alex,
"Are you ready to do this?"
Alex exclaimed,
"Yes! This is a Soccer Summer Dream!"

Walking beside my favorite player through the tunnel, his arm on my shoulder, I looked up at him with anticipation and the dream that one day I would be just like him - a professional soccer player. As we jogged onto the field with the bright lights shining from above, fireworks exploded in the sky as the fans proudly cheered and waved their Milwaukee Torrent team flags. We were then greeted by our competition. We exchanged a quick handshake and were ready to start the game. Feeling very nervous, I shifted my focus back to this once in a lifetime moment and remembered I had practiced, and I was prepared.

The entire game was full of excitement, close plays, and fancy footwork.

Then it happened... the defining moment!

Watching the game intently and just waiting to get in on the action, the midfielder passed the ball to the forward but it was deflected and headed out of bounds. At least that's what it looked like was happening. The other team took their eye off the ball, but I didn't. I acted quickly as I couldn't let it hit the wall.

I dashed and dove catching the soccer ball midair. With no time to waste, I fired it at Alex. She reacted with amazing speed and confidence and launched it like a rocket to the midfielder so he could take a quick throw in to the forward on the wing. It was the 90th minute of the game, the score was 2 - 2 and the seconds were ticking by. The Torrent dribbled the ball and attacked down field toward the goal. The forward crossed the ball into the middle where his teammate drove it with a bicycle kick into the upper 90.

GOAL!

The referee called the game, and the scoreboard flashed Milwaukee Torrent 3, opposing team 2. We won!

"We did it D!" Alex rushed toward me screaming.

The crowd erupted with cheers! The band played! The flags flew in victory! And the fireworks exploded in the night sky. The trophy was proudly presented to the Milwaukee Torrent!

And that's when the midfielder who scored the winning goal lifted Alex up onto his shoulders and carried her like the champion she was. He knew he couldn't have done it without her, without our teamwork. Then out of the blue, the Torrent goalie in celebration boosted me up on his shoulders too. We all made it happen together.

We did it! We won!

It truly was A Soccer Summer Dream... Come true!

The End

Be sure to check out all of Marla McKenna's books including:
Mom's Big Catch,
which can be customized to fit baseball teams,
Sadie's Big Steal,
I'm a Secret Superhero and
A Soccer Summer Dream With The Milwaukee Torrent.

www.marlamckenna.com

Partial proceeds from all of Marla's books benefit the Linda Blair WorldHeart Foundation, with special thanks to Rick Springfield for matching her donations. Help save a dog's life.
www.lindablairworldheart.org

Torrent Autographs

www.ingramcontent.com/pod-product-compliance
Lightning Source LLC
Chambersburg PA
CBHW041526070426

42452CB00035B/23